The following content is reproduced below with the goal of providing information that is as accurate and reliable as possible. Regardless, purchasing this content can be seen as consent to the fact that both the publisher and the author of this content are in no way experts on the topics discussed within and that any recommendations or suggestions that are made herein are for entertainment purposes only. Professionals should be consulted as needed prior to undertaking any of the action endorsed herein. This declaration is deemed fair and valid by both the American Bar Association and the Committee of Publishers Association and is legally binding throughout the United States.

Let the adventure begin...

make yourself proud.

People with medical conditions should consult their doctor before beginning the running program.

This workout plan consists of three running workouts per week. During the first 3 weeks, each workout lasts for 30 minutes and consists of alternating periods of progressive running and walking. During the next 7 weeks, the length of the workout increases from 40 to 60 minutes. The end goal is to gradually increase your running tolerance for up to 60 minutes.

Assuming 10 minutes/mile(km) pace you should be able to complete a 6,2-mile (10 kilometers) race at that time.

During this training period, it's important to listen to your body. If you start to experience pain take some time off and give it adequate time to heal and recover.

TYPES OF TRAINING

EASY RUN
You should be able to enjoy running without feeling tired.

STEADY RUN
You should be able to hold a conversation, but find it difficult.

TEMPO RUN
Constant speed running is sometimes referred to as tempo running. This improves your running pace. Aim to run at a constant speed that feels 'comfortably hard'.

WEEK 1

TIPS OF THE WEEK

Workout Time: **30min** Easy Run

Try to run the whole way. Take short walking breaks if necessary. Don't stop on your run if you are getting tired. Go slower or take a walking break instead of coming to a complete stop.

MONDAY

DATE & TIME: .... LOCATION: ....

DISTANCE: .... TIME: ....

HOW WAS YOUR RUN TODAY? (EASY) 1 2 3 4 5 (HARD)

YOUR NOTES: ....

TUESDAY

DATE: ....

TAKE A REST

HOW DO YOU FEEL TODAY? ....

....

WEDNESDAY

DATE & TIME: .... LOCATION: ....

DISTANCE: .... TIME: ....

HOW WAS YOUR RUN TODAY? (EASY) 1 2 3 4 5 (HARD)

YOUR NOTES: ....

Yes You Can

THURSDAY

DATE: ....

TAKE A REST

HOW DO YOU FEEL TODAY? ....

....

FRIDAY

DATE & TIME: .... LOCATION: ....

DISTANCE: .... TIME: ....

HOW WAS YOUR RUN TODAY? (EASY) 1 2 3 4 5 (HARD)

YOUR NOTES: ....

SATURDAY

DATE: ....

TAKE A REST

HOW DO YOU FEEL TODAY? ....

....

SUNDAY

DATE: ....

TAKE A REST

HOW DO YOU FEEL TODAY? ....

....

you are stronger than you think.

Find a familiar route for your runs. Use this same route for several days and if you're taking walking breaks try to run a little further each day until you can run the whole distance.

Don't be discouraged if you have to walk on the run for a few weeks. If you are new to running, it will take a little time to build your endurance. **Be patient!**

Feel free to tailor your training though. Just because the schedule says that you need to run x miles (km), or xx minutes, on one day doesn't mean that you can't make some adjustments to suit your lifestyle.

WEEK 2

TIPS OF THE WEEK

Workout Time: **30min** Easy Run

Try to run the whole way. Take short walking breaks if necessary. Don't stop on your run if you are getting tired. Go slower or take a walking break instead of coming to a complete stop.

MONDAY

DATE & TIME: .... LOCATION: ....

DISTANCE: .... TIME: ....

HOW WAS YOUR RUN TODAY?   (EASY) 1 2 3 4 5 (HARD)

YOUR NOTES: ....

TUESDAY

DATE: ....

TAKE A REST

HOW DO YOU FEEL TODAY? ....

....

WEDNESDAY

DATE & TIME: .... LOCATION: ....

DISTANCE: .... TIME: ....

HOW WAS YOUR RUN TODAY?   (EASY) 1 2 3 4 5 (HARD)

YOUR NOTES: ....

It's a RUNderful life

THURSDAY

DATE: ....

TAKE A REST

HOW DO YOU FEEL TODAY? ....

....

FRIDAY

DATE & TIME: .... LOCATION: ....

DISTANCE: .... TIME: ....

HOW WAS YOUR RUN TODAY? (EASY) 1 2 3 4 5 (HARD)

YOUR NOTES: ....

SATURDAY

DATE: ....

TAKE A REST

HOW DO YOU FEEL TODAY? ....

....

SUNDAY

DATE: ....

TAKE A REST

HOW DO YOU FEEL TODAY? ....

....

Notes

How do you feel?

WEEK 3

TIPS OF THE WEEK

Workout Time: **30min** Easy Run

Try to run the whole way. Take short walking breaks if necessary. Don't stop on your run if you are getting tired. Go slower or take a walking break instead of coming to a complete stop.

MONDAY

DATE & TIME: .... LOCATION: ....

DISTANCE: .... TIME: ....

HOW WAS YOUR RUN TODAY?   (EASY) 1 2 3 4 5 (HARD)

YOUR NOTES:
....

TUESDAY

DATE: ....

TAKE A REST

HOW DO YOU FEEL TODAY? ....

....

WEDNESDAY

DATE & TIME: .... LOCATION: ....

DISTANCE: .... TIME: ....

HOW WAS YOUR RUN TODAY?   (EASY) 1 2 3 4 5 (HARD)

YOUR NOTES:
....

You don't have to go fast

THURSDAY

DATE: ....

TAKE A REST

HOW DO YOU FEEL TODAY? ....

....

FRIDAY

DATE & TIME: .... LOCATION: ....

DISTANCE: .... TIME: ....

HOW WAS YOUR RUN TODAY? (EASY) 1 2 3 4 5 (HARD)

YOUR NOTES: ....

SATURDAY

DATE: ....

TAKE A REST

HOW DO YOU FEEL TODAY? ....

....

SUNDAY

DATE: ....

TAKE A REST

HOW DO YOU FEEL TODAY? ....

....

Notes

How do you feel?

WEEK 4

TIPS OF THE WEEK

Workout Time: **40min** Easy Run

Try to run the whole way. Please ensure you warm-up and cool down correctly at every workout. Your legs will start to feel stronger as you build muscles.

MONDAY

DATE & TIME: .... LOCATION: ....

DISTANCE: .... TIME: ....

HOW WAS YOUR RUN TODAY?   (EASY) 1 2 3 4 5 (HARD)

YOUR NOTES: ....

TUESDAY

DATE: ....

TAKE A REST

HOW DO YOU FEEL TODAY? ....

....

WEDNESDAY

DATE & TIME: .... LOCATION: ....

DISTANCE: .... TIME: ....

HOW WAS YOUR RUN TODAY?   (EASY) 1 2 3 4 5 (HARD)

YOUR NOTES: ....

Just Go

THURSDAY

DATE: ....

TAKE A REST

HOW DO YOU FEEL TODAY? ....

....

FRIDAY

DATE & TIME: .... LOCATION: ....

DISTANCE: .... TIME: ....

HOW WAS YOUR RUN TODAY?   (EASY) 1 2 3 4 5 (HARD)

YOUR NOTES: ....

SATURDAY

DATE: ....

TAKE A REST

HOW DO YOU FEEL TODAY? ....

....

SUNDAY

DATE: ....

TAKE A REST

HOW DO YOU FEEL TODAY? ....

....

Notes

How do you feel?

WEEK 5

TIPS OF THE WEEK

Workout Time: **40min** Steady Run

Try to run the whole way if you can. Listen to your body.

MONDAY

DATE & TIME: .... LOCATION: ....

DISTANCE: .... TIME: ....

HOW WAS YOUR RUN TODAY?   (EASY) 1   2   3   4   5 (HARD)

YOUR NOTES: ....

TUESDAY

DATE: ....

TAKE A REST

HOW DO YOU FEEL TODAY? ....

....

WEDNESDAY

DATE & TIME: .... LOCATION: ....

DISTANCE: .... TIME: ....

HOW WAS YOUR RUN TODAY?   (EASY) 1   2   3   4   5 (HARD)

YOUR NOTES: ....

Getting stronger each day

THURSDAY

DATE: ....

TAKE A REST

HOW DO YOU FEEL TODAY? ....

....

FRIDAY

DATE & TIME: .... LOCATION: ....

DISTANCE: .... TIME: ....

HOW WAS YOUR RUN TODAY? (EASY) 1 2 3 4 5 (HARD)

YOUR NOTES: ....

SATURDAY

DATE: ....

TAKE A REST

HOW DO YOU FEEL TODAY? ....

....

SUNDAY

DATE: ....

TAKE A REST

HOW DO YOU FEEL TODAY? ....

....

Notes

How do you feel?

WEEK 6

TIPS OF THE WEEK

Distance: **4 miles** (6,4 kilometres) Steady Run

Try to run the whole way if you can.
Listen to your body.

MONDAY

DATE & TIME: .... LOCATION: ....

DISTANCE: .... TIME: ....

HOW WAS YOUR RUN TODAY? (EASY) 1 2 3 4 5 (HARD)

YOUR NOTES: ....

TUESDAY

DATE: ....

TAKE A REST

HOW DO YOU FEEL TODAY? ....

....

WEDNESDAY

DATE & TIME: .... LOCATION: ....

DISTANCE: .... TIME: ....

HOW WAS YOUR RUN TODAY? (EASY) 1 2 3 4 5 (HARD)

YOUR NOTES: ....

Run and be Happy

THURSDAY

DATE: ....

TAKE A REST

HOW DO YOU FEEL TODAY? ....

....

FRIDAY

DATE & TIME: .... LOCATION: ....

DISTANCE: .... TIME: ....

HOW WAS YOUR RUN TODAY?   (EASY) 1 2 3 4 5 (HARD)

YOUR NOTES: ....

SATURDAY

DATE: ....

TAKE A REST

HOW DO YOU FEEL TODAY? ....

....

SUNDAY

DATE: ....

TAKE A REST

HOW DO YOU FEEL TODAY? ....

....

Notes

How do you feel?

WEEK 7

TIPS OF THE WEEK

Distance: **4 miles** (6,4 kilometres) Tempo Run

Try to run the whole way if you can.
Listen to your body.

MONDAY

DATE & TIME: .... LOCATION: ....

DISTANCE: .... TIME: ....

HOW WAS YOUR RUN TODAY?   (EASY) 1 2 3 4 5 (HARD)

YOUR NOTES: ....

TUESDAY

DATE: ....

TAKE A REST

HOW DO YOU FEEL TODAY? ....

....

WEDNESDAY

DATE & TIME: .... LOCATION: ....

DISTANCE: .... TIME: ....

HOW WAS YOUR RUN TODAY?   (EASY) 1 2 3 4 5 (HARD)

YOUR NOTES: ....

Run for Your Life

THURSDAY

DATE: ....

TAKE A REST

HOW DO YOU FEEL TODAY? ....

....

FRIDAY

DATE & TIME: ....   LOCATION: ....

DISTANCE: ....   TIME: ....

HOW WAS YOUR RUN TODAY?   (EASY) 1   2   3   4   5   (HARD)

YOUR NOTES: ....

SATURDAY

DATE: ....

TAKE A REST

HOW DO YOU FEEL TODAY? ....

....

SUNDAY

DATE: ....

TAKE A REST

HOW DO YOU FEEL TODAY? ....

....

Notes

How do you feel?

WEEK 8

TIPS OF THE WEEK

Distance: **5 miles** (8 kilometres) Easy Run

Try to run the whole way if you can.
Listen to your body.

MONDAY

DATE & TIME: .... LOCATION: ....

DISTANCE: .... TIME: ....

HOW WAS YOUR RUN TODAY?   (EASY) 1 2 3 4 5 (HARD)

YOUR NOTES: ....

TUESDAY

DATE: ....

TAKE A REST

HOW DO YOU FEEL TODAY? ....

....

WEDNESDAY

DATE & TIME: .... LOCATION: ....

DISTANCE: .... TIME: ....

HOW WAS YOUR RUN TODAY?   (EASY) 1 2 3 4 5 (HARD)

YOUR NOTES: ....

It's fine. I Run today

THURSDAY

DATE: ....

TAKE A REST

HOW DO YOU FEEL TODAY? ....

....

FRIDAY

DATE & TIME: .... LOCATION: ....

DISTANCE: .... TIME: ....

HOW WAS YOUR RUN TODAY?   (EASY) 1   2   3   4   5   (HARD)

YOUR NOTES: ....

SATURDAY

DATE: ....

TAKE A REST

HOW DO YOU FEEL TODAY? ....

....

SUNDAY

DATE: ....

TAKE A REST

HOW DO YOU FEEL TODAY? ....

....

Notes

How do you feel?

WEEK 9

TIPS OF THE WEEK

Distance: **5 miles** (8 kilometres) Steady Run

Try to run the whole way if you can.
Listen to your body.

MONDAY

DATE & TIME: .... LOCATION: ....

DISTANCE: .... TIME: ....

HOW WAS YOUR RUN TODAY? (EASY) 1 2 3 4 5 (HARD)

YOUR NOTES: ....

TUESDAY

DATE: ....

TAKE A REST

HOW DO YOU FEEL TODAY? ....

....

WEDNESDAY

DATE & TIME: .... LOCATION: ....

DISTANCE: .... TIME: ....

HOW WAS YOUR RUN TODAY? (EASY) 1 2 3 4 5 (HARD)

YOUR NOTES: ....

BlaBlaBla Go workout

THURSDAY

DATE: ....

TAKE A REST

HOW DO YOU FEEL TODAY? ....

....

FRIDAY

DATE & TIME: .... LOCATION: ....

DISTANCE: .... TIME: ....

HOW WAS YOUR RUN TODAY? (EASY) 1 2 3 4 5 (HARD)

YOUR NOTES: ....

SATURDAY

DATE: ....

TAKE A REST

HOW DO YOU FEEL TODAY? ....

....

SUNDAY

DATE: ....

TAKE A REST

HOW DO YOU FEEL TODAY? ....

....

Notes

How do you feel?

WEEK 10

TIPS OF THE WEEK

Monday/Wednesday: **6,2 miles** (10 kilometres) Easy Run
Friday: **6,2 miles** (10 kilometres) Steady Run

Try to run the whole way if you can.
Listen to your body.

MONDAY

DATE & TIME: .... LOCATION: ....

DISTANCE: .... TIME: ....

HOW WAS YOUR RUN TODAY? (EASY) 1 2 3 4 5 (HARD)

YOUR NOTES: ....

TUESDAY

DATE: ....

TAKE A REST

HOW DO YOU FEEL TODAY? ....

....

WEDNESDAY

DATE & TIME: .... LOCATION: ....

DISTANCE: .... TIME: ....

HOW WAS YOUR RUN TODAY? (EASY) 1 2 3 4 5 (HARD)

YOUR NOTES: ....

Today is The Day

THURSDAY

DATE: ....

TAKE A REST

HOW DO YOU FEEL TODAY? ....

....

FRIDAY

DATE & TIME: .... LOCATION: ....

DISTANCE: .... TIME: ....

HOW WAS YOUR RUN TODAY? (EASY) 1 2 3 4 5 (HARD)

YOUR NOTES: ....

SATURDAY

DATE: ....

TAKE A REST

HOW DO YOU FEEL TODAY? ....

....

SUNDAY

DATE: ....

TAKE A REST

HOW DO YOU FEEL TODAY? ....

....

great.

How do you feel?

RUNNING LOG

DATE	DISTANCE	TIME	PACE	NOTES

RUNNING LOG

DATE	DISTANCE	TIME	PACE	NOTES

RUNNING LOG

DATE	DISTANCE	TIME	PACE	NOTES

RUNNING LOG

DATE	DISTANCE	TIME	PACE	NOTES

RUNNING LOG

DATE	DISTANCE	TIME	PACE	NOTES

RUNNING LOG

DATE	DISTANCE	TIME	PACE	NOTES

RUNNING LOG

DATE	DISTANCE	TIME	PACE	NOTES

RUNNING LOG

DATE	DISTANCE	TIME	PACE	NOTES

RUNNING LOG

DATE	DISTANCE	TIME	PACE	NOTES

RUNNING LOG

DATE	DISTANCE	TIME	PACE	NOTES

RUNNING LOG

DATE	DISTANCE	TIME	PACE	NOTES

RUNNING LOG

DATE	DISTANCE	TIME	PACE	NOTES

RUNNING LOG

DATE	DISTANCE	TIME	PACE	NOTES

RUNNING LOG

DATE	DISTANCE	TIME	PACE	NOTES

RUNNING LOG

DATE	DISTANCE	TIME	PACE	NOTES

RUNNING LOG

DATE	DISTANCE	TIME	PACE	NOTES

RUNNING LOG

DATE	DISTANCE	TIME	PACE	NOTES

RUNNING LOG

DATE	DISTANCE	TIME	PACE	NOTES

RUNNING LOG

DATE	DISTANCE	TIME	PACE	NOTES

RUNNING LOG

DATE	DISTANCE	TIME	PACE	NOTES

RUNNING LOG

DATE	DISTANCE	TIME	PACE	NOTES

RUNNING LOG

DATE	DISTANCE	TIME	PACE	NOTES

RUNNING LOG

DATE	DISTANCE	TIME	PACE	NOTES

RUNNING LOG

DATE	DISTANCE	TIME	PACE	NOTES

RUNNING LOG

DATE	DISTANCE	TIME	PACE	NOTES

RUNNING LOG

DATE	DISTANCE	TIME	PACE	NOTES

RUNNING LOG

DATE	DISTANCE	TIME	PACE	NOTES

RUNNING LOG

DATE	DISTANCE	TIME	PACE	NOTES

RUNNING LOG

DATE	DISTANCE	TIME	PACE	NOTES

RUNNING LOG

DATE	DISTANCE	TIME	PACE	NOTES

RUNNING LOG

DATE	DISTANCE	TIME	PACE	NOTES

RUNNING LOG

DATE	DISTANCE	TIME	PACE	NOTES

RUNNING LOG

DATE	DISTANCE	TIME	PACE	NOTES

RUNNING LOG

DATE	DISTANCE	TIME	PACE	NOTES

RUNNING LOG

DATE	DISTANCE	TIME	PACE	NOTES

RUNNING LOG

DATE	DISTANCE	TIME	PACE	NOTES

RUNNING LOG

DATE	DISTANCE	TIME	PACE	NOTES

RUNNING LOG

DATE	DISTANCE	TIME	PACE	NOTES

RUNNING LOG

DATE	DISTANCE	TIME	PACE	NOTES

RUNNING LOG

DATE	DISTANCE	TIME	PACE	NOTES

RUNNING LOG

DATE	DISTANCE	TIME	PACE	NOTES

RUNNING LOG

DATE	DISTANCE	TIME	PACE	NOTES

RUNNING LOG

DATE	DISTANCE	TIME	PACE	NOTES

RUNNING LOG

DATE	DISTANCE	TIME	PACE	NOTES

RUNNING LOG

DATE	DISTANCE	TIME	PACE	NOTES

RUNNING LOG

DATE	DISTANCE	TIME	PACE	NOTES

RUNNING LOG

DATE	DISTANCE	TIME	PACE	NOTES

RUNNING LOG

DATE	DISTANCE	TIME	PACE	NOTES

RUNNING LOG

DATE	DISTANCE	TIME	PACE	NOTES

RUNNING LOG

DATE	DISTANCE	TIME	PACE	NOTES

RUNNING LOG

DATE	DISTANCE	TIME	PACE	NOTES

RUNNING LOG

DATE	DISTANCE	TIME	PACE	NOTES

RUNNING LOG

DATE	DISTANCE	TIME	PACE	NOTES

RUNNING LOG

DATE	DISTANCE	TIME	PACE	NOTES

Made in the USA
Coppell, TX
27 December 2019